Variations and Fugue
on a Theme by Handel

Op.24

By

Johannes Brahms

For Solo Piano

1861

British Library Cataloguing-in-Publication Data
A catalogue record for this book is available from
the British Library

Variationen und Fuge
über ein Thema von Händel für Pianoforte

Johannes Brahms, Op.24
(Veröffentlicht 1862)

Var. 2

Var. 8

Var. 11

Var. 14

Var. 17

più mosso

Var. 18

grazioso

Var. 21

Var. 24

Var. 25

Fuga

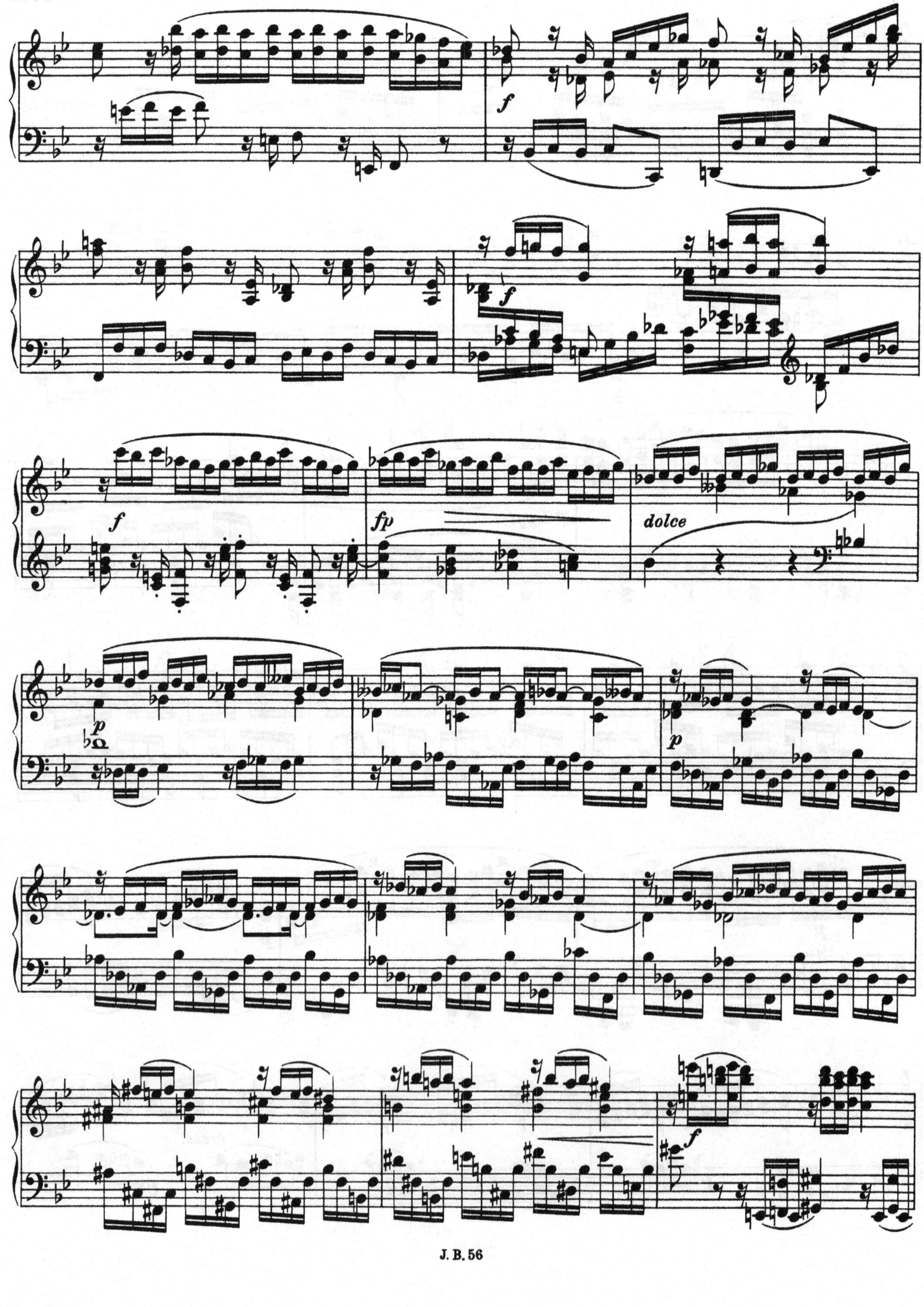
f
f
f
fp
dolce
p
p
f

Lightning Source UK Ltd.
Milton Keynes UK
UKOW07f0631070118

315596UK00024B/395/P

9 781447 475736